IF ANIMALS COULD TALK

BY CARLA BUTWIN
& JOSH CASSIDY

STERLING
New York

STERLING
New York

An Imprint of Sterling Publishing
1166 Avenue of the Americas
New York, NY 10036

ISBN 978-1-4549-1939-1

Distributed in Canada by Sterling Publishing
c/o Canadian Manda Group, 664 Annette Street
Toronto, Ontario, Canada M6S 2C8
Distributed in the United Kingdom by GMC Distribution Services
Castle Place, 166 High Street, Lewes, East Sussex, England BN7 1XU
Distributed in Australia by Capricorn Link (Australia) Pty. Ltd.
P.O. Box 704, Windsor, NSW 2756, Australia

For information about custom editions, special sales, and premium and corporate purchases, please contact Sterling Special Sales at 800-805-5489 or specialsales@sterlingpublishing.com.

Manufactured in China

2 4 6 8 10 9 7 5 3 1

www.sterlingpublishing.com

"MY COUSIN IS A RUG."
-ALPACA

"STHOP MAKING FUN
OF MY LITHP."
-SNAKE

"IT'S HOT AS BALLS IN HERE."
-ANGORA RABBIT

"BAD BITCHES ONLY."
-POODLE

"IF YOU DRESS ME UP ONE
MORE TIME I'M GOING TO
MURDER YOUR FAMILY."
-GUINEA PIG

"I'LL...GET...THERE...WHEN...I...GET...THERE!"
-SNAIL

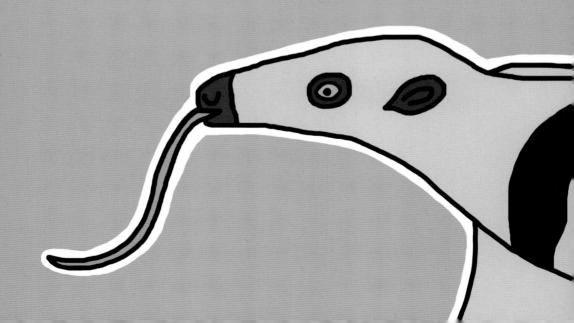

"YAAAA FAMILY REUNIONS SUCK."
-BLACK SHEEP

"I'M NOT MUCH OF A CUDDLER."
-SCORPION

"FUCK SHARK WEEK."
-GRAY WHALE

"MAKIN' IT RAIN
ON DEM HOES."
-PIGEON

"BYE FELICIA."
-PERSIAN CAT

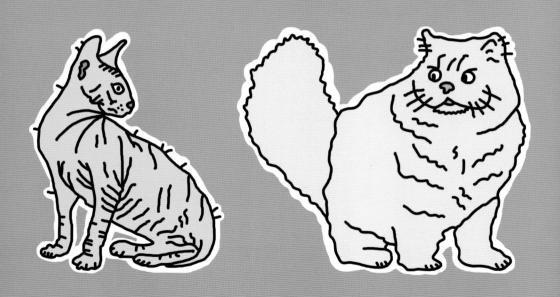

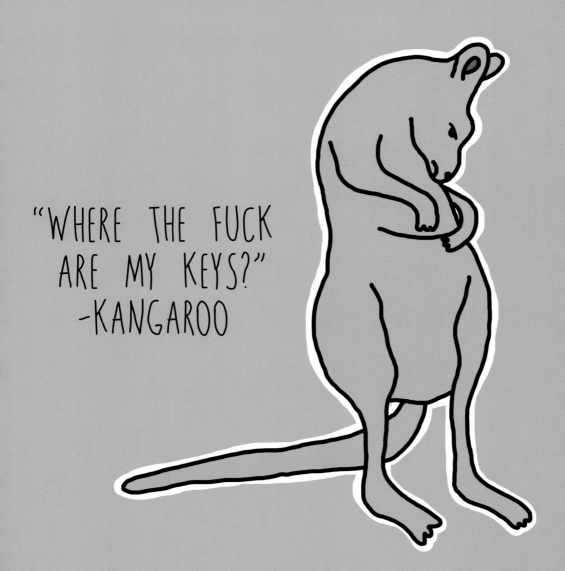

"WHERE THE FUCK
ARE MY KEYS?"
-KANGAROO

"PIZZAAAAA!"
-DOG

"NEXT TIME, I'M GETTING DELIVERY."
-RAT

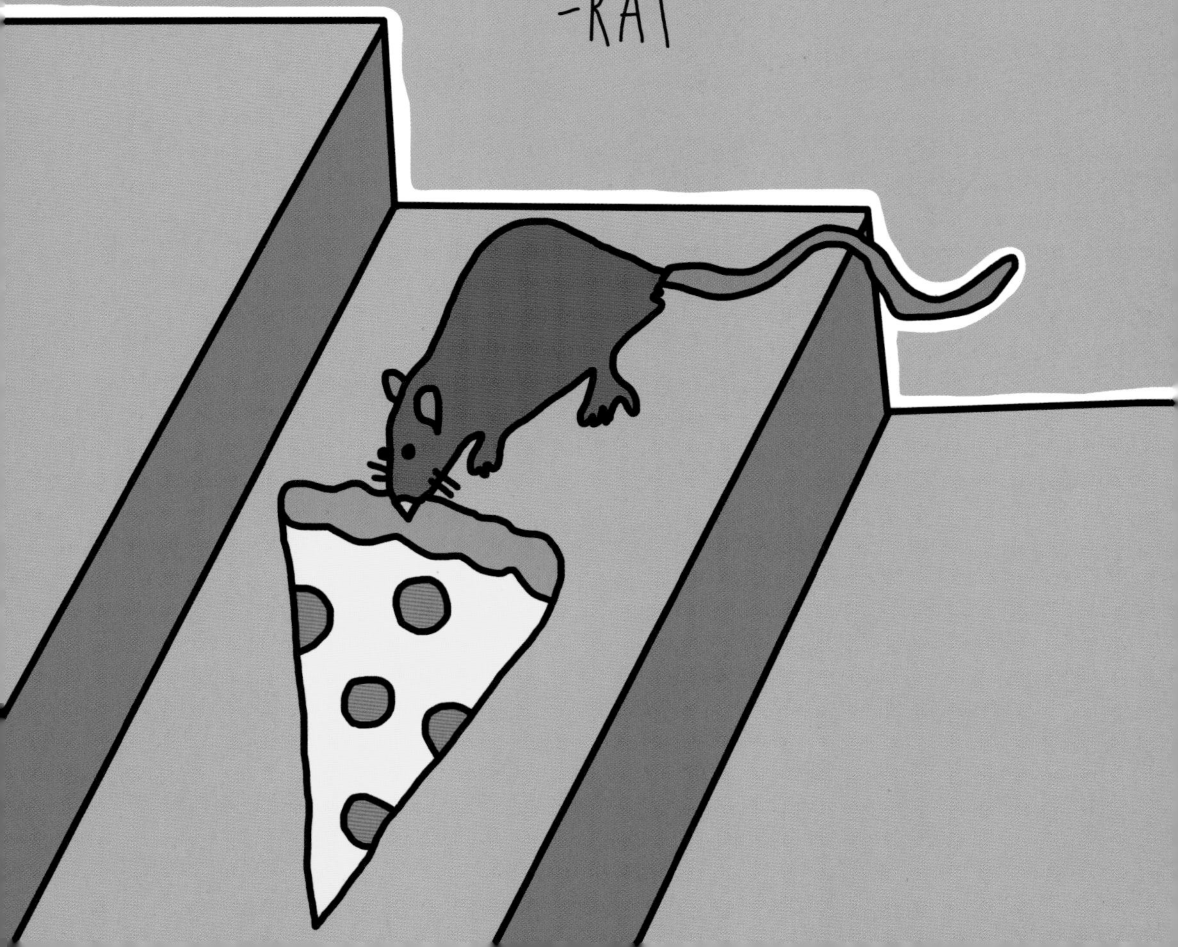

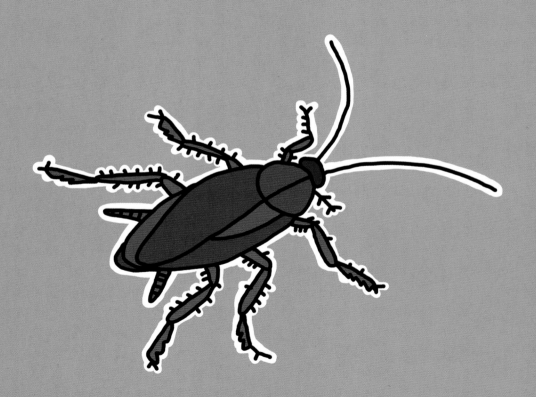

"BRO, I DIDN'T
TOUCH YOUR
SALMON."
-GRIZZLY BEAR

"WHO WANTS A HICKEY?"
-LEECH

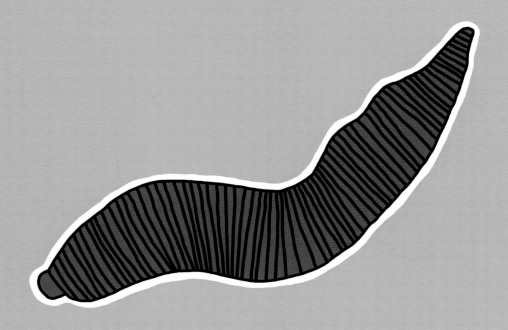

"AND YOU THOUGHT KIDS MADE FUN OF YOUR NAME."
-DIK-DIK

"NO, I DON'T PLAY BASKETBALL."
-GIRAFFE

"YOU GIVE THE REST
OF US A BAD NAME."
-PIT BULL TO PITBULL

"DUDE, THIS IS SOME GOOD SHIT."
-FLY

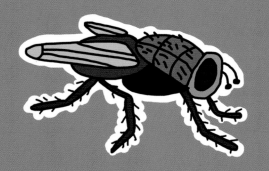 

"MY REAL NAME IS CLARENCE."
-FLIPPER

"I SEE DEAD PEOPLE."
-WORM

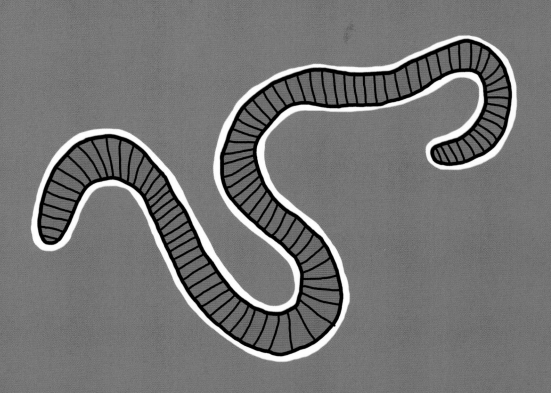

"WHAT KIND OF
SORCERY IS THIS?"
-CAT

"YO, MY PERIPHERAL GAME
IS ON POINT."
-HAMMERHEAD SHARK

"ALL MY SHIT DESIGNER."
-PEACOCK

"OOPS."
-JELLYFISH

"MY PRECIOUS..."
-SQUIRREL

"BLURBBBRLBBUBBLRR."
-BLOBFISH

"YOU DON'T LOOK LIKE YOUR PROFILE PIC EITHER."
-CATFISH

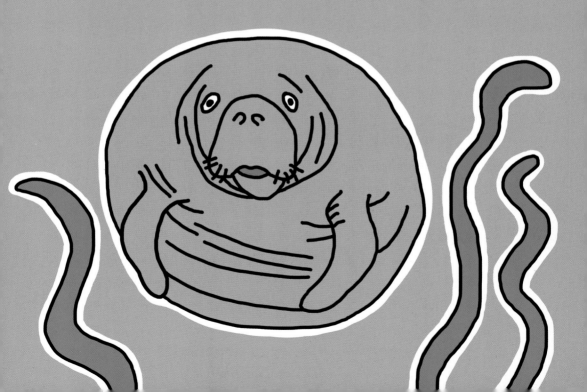

"PLASTIC SURGERY IS
A SLIPPERY SLOPE."
-PLATYPUS

"YOU MUTHA FUCKAS
TRYIN' TO JOUST?"
-NARWHALE

"WITCHES AIN'T SHIT
BUT HOES N' TRICKS."
-BLACK CAT

"BALL IS LIFE."
-HAMSTER

"LEBRON SSSSSSUCKS."
-BLACK MAMBA

"I CAN'T FEEL MY FACE."
-KOALA

"OH, YEAH? WELL YOU
LOOK LIKE A VAGINA."
-WEINER DOG

"BITCH, TOUCH ME
AND SEE WHAT HAPPENS."
-POISON DART FROG

"YOU MAKE EVERY
DAY FEEL LIKE
TACO TUESDAY."
-OTTER

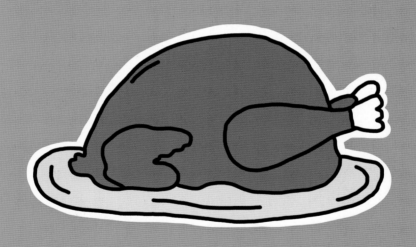

"SOMEONE GET MY EPIPEN!"
-BLOWFISH

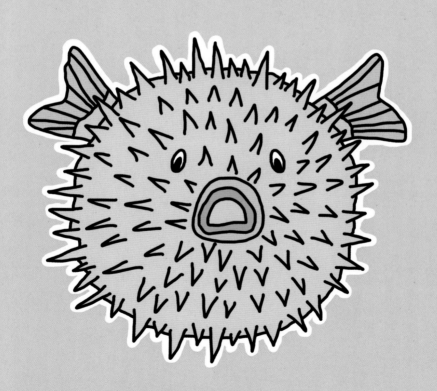

"DAMN, I NEED TO GET MY NAILS DID."
-SLOTH

"I BELIEVE I CAN FLY."
-PIG

"WELL, THIS IS GONNA BE AWKWARD."
-RABBIT

"A SPEEDING TICKET?
ARE YOU FUCKING KIDDING ME?"
-TURTLE

THE END

"THANKS TO ALL OF OUR FAMILY,
FRIENDS AND FOLLOWERS.
WITHOUT YOUR SUPPORT AND INSPIRATION,
THIS BOOK WOULD NEVER BE.
YOU DA BEST."
-CARLA & JOSH

Carla Butwin and **Josh Cassidy** are the artists behind *If Animals Could Talk*.
They met as Junior Creatives at a Detroit ad agency and have since turned
their friendship into a bi-coastal creative partnership. One day, Josh (LA) started
randomly writing jokes in the form of animal quotes and coincidentally discovered
that Carla (NY) really liked drawing animals in her free time. Weird, right?
They soon began collaborating and created a blog as a fun outlet from their day
jobs. Thousands of followers later, they're now applying their college degrees and
years of professional creative experience to write books about talking animals.

GOT ANIMALS
YOU WANT TO SEE TALK?
LET US KNOW.

@ifblankcouldtalk on Instagram.
ifblankcouldtalk.com on Tumblr.